NATURAL WORLD

GIANT
PANDA

HABITATS • LIFE CYCLES • FOOD CHAINS • THREATS

Malcolm Penny

WAYLAND

WWF

Produced in Association with WWF-UK

NATURAL WORLD

Chimpanzee • Crocodile • Dolphin • Elephant • Giant Panda
Great White Shark • Killer Whale • Lion • Orangutan
Penguin • Polar Bear • Tiger

Produced for Wayland Publishers Limited by
Roger Coote Publishing
Gissing's Farm, Fressingfield
Suffolk IP21 5SH, UK

First published in 1999 by
Wayland Publishers Limited
61 Western Road, Hove
East Sussex BN3 1JD, England

All Wayland books encourage children to read and help them
improve their literacy.

✓ The contents page, page numbers, headings and index
help locate specific pieces of information.

✓ The glossary reinforces alphabetic knowledge and
extends vocabulary.

✓ The further information section suggests other books
dealing with the same subject.

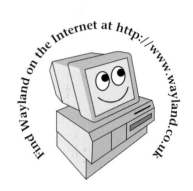

find Wayland on the Internet at http://www.wayland.co.uk

Cover: Face to face with the giant panda.
Title page: Bamboo is the panda's main food.
Contents page: A young panda clings to a branch.
Index page: A panda enjoys a light snack.

WWF is a registered charity no. 201707
WWF-UK, Panda House, Weyside Park
Godalming, Surrey GU7 1XR

British Library Cataloguing in Publication Data
Penny, Malcolm
  Giant panda: habitats, life cycles, food chains,
  threats. – (Natural world)
  1. Giant panda - Juvenile literature
  I. Title
  599.7'89

ISBN 0 7502 2449 5

Picture acknowledgements
Bruce Coleman Collection 9 (Sophy & Michael
Day), 11 (Rod Williams), 14 (Clive Hicks), 15
(Gerald S Cubitt), 16 (Rod Williams), 18 (Hans
Reinhard), 23 (Sophy & Michael Day), 27, 30
(Hans Reinhard), 31 (Hans Reinhard), 35 (Sophy &
Michael Day), 37 (Mark Carwardine), 42 (Hans
Reinhard), 45 middle (Sophy & Michael Day), 45
bottom (Hans Reinhard), 48 (Erwin & Peggy
Bauer); Heather Angel/Biofotos 1, 3, 6, 7, 10,
12–13, 13, 17, 20, 21, 22, 24, 25, 26, 28, 29, 32, 33,
34, 38, 39, 40, 41, 44 top, 44 bottom, 45 top; Still
Pictures 8 (Roland Seitre), 36 (Roland Seitre), 43
(Roland Seitre), 44 middle (Roland Seitre); Tony
Stone Images *front cover* (Keren Su).
Maps on page 4 by Victoria Webb and Peter Bull.
All other artwork by Michael Posen.

Printed and bound by G. Canale & C. S.p.A., Turin, Italy

Contents

Meet the Giant Panda 4

A Panda is Born 8

Growing Up 14

Leaving Home 30

Threats 36

Panda Life Cycle 44

Topic Web 46

Extension Activities 46

Glossary 47

Further Information 47

Index 48

Meet the Giant Panda

The giant panda is one of the most popular and easily recognized mammals in the world. Sadly, it also one of the rarest. This large, shy, stocky creature is a black-and-white relative of bears.

The giant panda is in great danger of becoming extinct. It is found in the wild in just three provinces of China – Sichuan, Shaanxi and Gansu.

◀ China's position in the world.

CHINA

▲ The red areas on this map show where giant pandas live in the wild.

PANDA FACTS

The giant panda's Latin name, *Ailuropoda melanoleuca*, means 'cat-footed black and white'.

●

A giant panda measures 70–80 centimetres tall at the shoulder when on all four legs, and 170 centimetres when standing upright. It weighs 100–150 kilograms. Males are usually about 10 per cent larger than females.

▶ An adult giant panda.

Front paws
The wrist bone of each front paw is enlarged to form a 'false thumb'. The panda grips bamboo by pressing the first two claws against its false thumb.

Head
The panda's skull is very heavy. The powerful chewing muscles that operate the jaws are anchored to the cheekbones.

Eyes
The panda's sensitive eyes, with their vertical pupils, give it good night vision.

Legs
Stout legs carry the weight of the panda's heavy body.

Teeth
The giant panda has no shearing or incisor teeth for slicing through flesh. Most of its teeth are molars, which are broad to grind up food such as tough bamboo stems. It also has large canine teeth, with which it can defend itself.

Feet
Pads at the base of the claws (see above) improve the panda's grip. The feet are covered in thick hair, which helps the panda walk over snow and ice.

The Panda's Habitat

The giant panda lives in China's remote mountain forests, 2,600–3,500 metres above sea-level, where the mountain air is very thin. Some scientists think that the panda's blood is specially adapted to carry extra oxygen, so that it can survive at these high altitudes.

At the upper levels of the forests, tall conifer trees are interspersed with rhododendrons and scattered clumps of slender bamboo about a metre high. Lower down the mountain slopes, where the forest is thicker, dense clumps of bamboo up to 3 metres tall are found between the mixture of conifers and deciduous trees.

▶ In the mountains of China, the temperature rarely rises above 20 °C, and in winter it can fall to as low as –7 °C.

▲ The giant panda shares its cold, misty habitat with many other forest animals, including red pandas.

RED PANDAS

The red panda is a smaller, more nimble animal than the giant panda, and a better climber. Like the panda, it has a false thumb. It has similar teeth to the panda and may also have specially adapted blood. Despite this, most scientists now agree that the two species are not closely related. The giant panda is a bear, while the red panda is related to raccoons. The similarities between the two types of panda occur because both animals are bamboo-eaters that live at high altitude.

A Panda is Born

Female pandas breed every two or three years. After mating, a female panda is pregnant for between 96 and 168 days. She looks for a place to make a den where she can give birth, such as at the base of a large, hollow tree. Then she lines it with leafy branches and clumps of vegetation.

A panda mother is about 900 times heavier than her new-born cub, which weighs 90–130 grams. At birth, the cub is about the size of a rat. It is pink, blind and completely helpless.

▲ Newborn giant panda cubs in a breeding centre in China. One of these cubs died at five days old, but her brother (above) survived. In the top photo he is ten days old.

Giant pandas usually have one or two cubs, or very rarely three. The mother will almost always rear one of her cubs and ignore any others, which soon die. This is probably because a new-born cub needs constant attention during the first few weeks of life. It wriggles about when it is fed, and has to be held firmly by its mother.

▼ A mother cleans her ten-week-old cub in a breeding centre in China.

Early Days

For the first week of its life, a giant panda cub is fed by its mother every hour. The cub sucks milk from its mother's teats. When feeding is over, she then spends about fifteen minutes licking the cub clean. The mother cradles her cub with her forepaws most of the time during the first three weeks.

While it is small, the cub is in great danger from a wide range of predators, including stoats, weasels, martens, golden cats and leopards. After two weeks, the cub looks rather like a piglet, but the pattern of its fur is beginning to show.

▲ A mother cleans her six-month-old cub's fur.

▶ China's mountain forests are also home to the beautiful golden cat, which is a serious threat to baby pandas.

Development and Danger

A giant panda cub develops very slowly. It does not open its eyes for the first six or eight weeks, and cannot crawl until it is two-and-a-half or three months. By the age of four months, when it weighs about four kilograms, the cub can walk on its own.

After about eight months, the cub is weaned and starts to eat its first stems of bamboo. The cub may get infested by parasitic worms, such as roundworms, which are found on food and in the soil. The worms live inside the panda's gut and can make it very ill. They may even cause it to die.

▼ At first, panda cubs are very vulnerable. By the time they are about a year old, like this cub, they can defend themselves against all but the largest predators.

The cub can now defend itself against small predators, such as stoats and weasels, using its sharp claws and large canine teeth. If bigger predators threaten, it climbs quickly into a tree to escape.

▲ Young pandas are good climbers, and will scramble up the nearest tree trunk if they sense danger approaching.

13

Growing Up

The cub normally stays with its mother until it is at least eighteen months old, and sometimes for three years or more. It follows its mother through the forest, learning from her where to find the best food plants at different times of the year.

▲ A panda nestles in a clump of bamboo. Different kinds of bamboo are good to eat at different times of the year.

One of the first things the panda cub learns about forest life is not to waste valuable energy struggling up and down steep slopes through dense undergrowth. Pandas usually walk along gentle, well-trodden paths made by deer and other forest animals.

Other Forest Dwellers

As it gets to know the forest, the young panda meets red pandas and many other animals, including tragopan and monal pheasants. These birds are brightly coloured to enable them to find each other in the gloomy forest.

▼ Tragopans are one of nine species of colourful pheasant that can be found in the forests of China.

Troops of golden monkeys live in the treetops. They have thick, shining coats and blue faces. On the forest floor are porcupines and musk deer. Musk deer have no antlers but defend themselves with long, tusk-like teeth that protrude from their upper lip.

But danger lurks in the depths of the forest, too. Young cubs must watch out for large predators. Leopards will sometimes prey on panda cubs, but dholes are the cub's worst natural enemy. Dholes are hunting dogs that live in packs of between five and twelve animals. They have been known to kill and eat old pandas as well as young cubs.

▲ A male musk deer has visible tusks. The female's tusks do not show outside her mouth.

MUSK DEER

Musk deer are often hunted for their scent glands. The oily liquid from the gland is used in traditional Chinese medicine to treat a wide range of diseases, and also in the West to make expensive perfumes. To collect 1 kilogram of the liquid, which can sell for as much as £30,000, about 70 deer have to be killed.

A female golden ▶ snub-nosed monkey with her baby. Males sometimes leap down from the trees from as high as 30 metres, breaking branches as they fall to the ground.

Food and Feeding

Like its mother, the young panda is soon eating mainly arrow bamboo, which grows on the lower slopes of the mountain. Pandas wander from clump to clump, selecting a few shoots here and there. They often smell them carefully before they eat them, which may help them decide which are the best shoots to eat.

▼ No one is sure why pandas spend so much time deciding which shoots to eat.

A panda might sit feeding for an hour in one place, or wander to a new feeding spot after a few minutes.

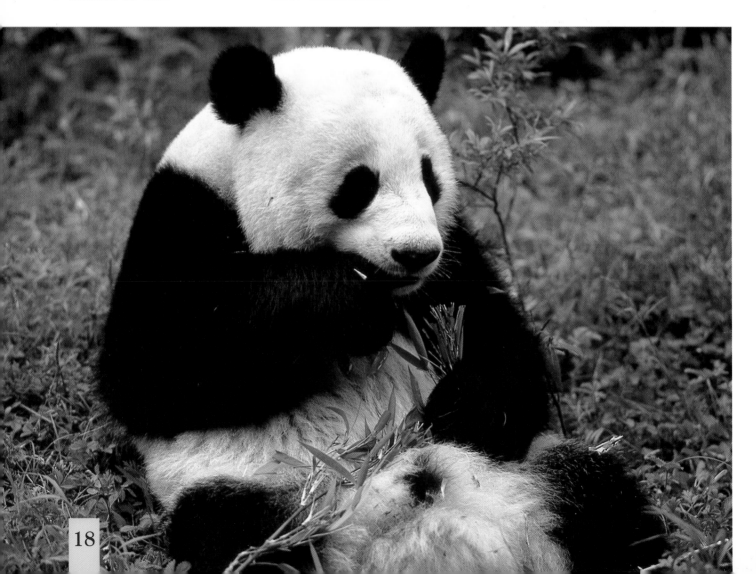

GIANT PANDA FOOD CHAIN

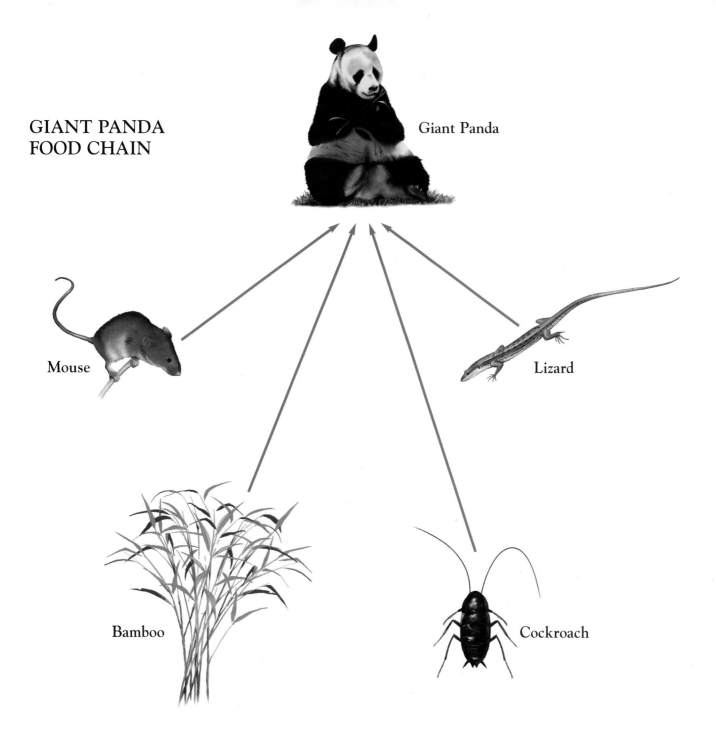

Giant Panda

Mouse

Lizard

Bamboo

Cockroach

▲ Adult giant pandas are at the top of their food chain. Pandas sometimes eat things other than bamboo, including insects and small rodents and reptiles.

Umbrella bamboo is a tasty panda delicacy that grows new shoots in May and June. The pandas specially seek out this type of bamboo. They eat only the plant's soft shoots and avoid the tougher leaves. Some other animals avoid the leaves, too, which suggests that they might be difficult to digest, or even poisonous at this time of year.

How Pandas Eat

When a giant panda feeds, it sits up on its haunches and lifts the bamboo to its mouth with one forepaw. It chews leaves and shoots very carefully, but only roughly crunches up the stems, so that its droppings afterwards contain a mass of splinters. The panda's gut has a tough lining to protect it against swallowed splinters.

Arrow bamboo is easy to eat. The panda holds the stem in one paw and bites pieces off, just as we might eat a stick of celery. However, umbrella bamboo is not so easy, because its shoots have a tough, bristly outer casing, which the panda strips off with its teeth before eating the shoot.

▲ A panda's false thumb helps it to grip the slender bamboo stems firmly as it eats.

Bamboo is plentiful in the forest, but it is low in energy-giving carbohydrates, so an adult giant panda must eat a vast amount to get the energy it needs. An adult panda will consume about 650 shoots a day, weighing about 38 kilograms – a quarter of its own body weight.

▼ This giant panda is using its tongue to strip the leaves off a bamboo shoot.

When the Bamboo Flowers

Bamboo is a type of grass. Like other grasses, it dies once it has flowered and produced seeds. Some small bamboo species flower every year, but larger species may have a flowering cycle of up to 120 years.

Arrow bamboo, the panda's main source of food, flowers every forty to fifty years. When flowering takes place, it can be a disaster for the pandas. As soon as the bamboo plants in a particular area have seeded, they all die off at once, leaving the pandas with nothing to eat.

▼ A panda carefully chews up bamboo leaves, including their stems, before swallowing them.

To avoid starving to death, the pandas must move to a place where there is enough food to keep them alive until new bamboo shoots appear. They either travel to parts of the mountain where the arrow bamboo has not yet flowered, or to the valleys, where different species of bamboo grow.

Pandas that are too old or sick to make the journey will die, but the rest will survive.

▲ When the bamboo flowers and goes to seed, it is a time of feasting for many seed-eating animals. But pandas risk starvation, and they may have to travel long distances in search of food.

23

▲ Pandas sometimes eat tree bark. The bark may contain vitamins that are not found in other kinds of food.

Other Food

Although pandas mainly eat bamboo, they will sometimes feed on bulbs, herbs, tree bark and even meat. Pandas do catch and eat large insects and small rodents and reptiles. There are even reports of a panda catching fish.

Panda droppings have also been found containing the bones of golden monkeys and musk deer. But it is unlikely that a heavy panda could have chased and caught these nimble animals. The panda probably found them when they were already dead.

Poachers and scientists sometimes use smoked meat to lure pandas into traps. This may be more a sign of the panda's curiosity about strange scents in the forest than its taste for such food.

Pandas get most of the water they need from their diet of juicy bamboo shoots. They sometimes make a drinking pool for themselves by digging a hole by a stream and waiting for it to fill with water.

▼ Although pandas usually get their water by eating bamboo, they may also lick snow to increase their intake of water.

Pandas make a variety of different sounds to communicate with each other. Low, growling notes travel farthest through the thick forest.

Communication

The young panda must learn how to communicate with other pandas. Although they are usually silent, pandas have a wide range of calls for special occasions. A small cub cries like a human baby, with a high-pitched call that is impossible for a parent to ignore.

During the breeding season, a female stands on a high ridge and produces deep roars, barks and moans that can be heard in neighbouring valleys. When she is ready to mate, she utters a strange bleating call, rather like a goat.

Pandas also communicate with each other with their body scent and strong-smelling urine, which they use to mark out the areas where they live.

▶ Unlike the rest of the bear family, pandas do not use facial expressions to communicate. When one panda wants to threaten another, it simply stares at its rival with its head down, perhaps so that its black ears look like another pair of eyes against the white fur of its neck.

A Giant Panda's Day

Since they live in forests on steep hillsides, giant pandas are very hard to study. By fitting them with special collars that give out radio signals, scientists have been able to find out what they do and where they go, and what a typical day in the life of a panda is like.

For most of its waking hours, a panda moves between clumps of bamboo looking for food. It feeds both day and night, but is most active in the early morning and late afternoon. Pandas normally rest for between two and four hours between meals, but in summer they rest for longer, sometimes sleeping for six hours or more.

▼ Pandas can sometimes be seen rolling down slopes. It is possible that this is just a playful act, but it may have a more practical use, such as to dislodge twigs from their fur.

▲ This panda is resting with its head propped on a tree root, to keep it away from the freezing ground.

With its thick, oily coat, a panda has little need to seek shelter, except in the heaviest rain, when it might retreat into a hollow tree or a cave. The panda rarely grooms its fur, but keeps it in good condition by rolling on the ground and rubbing soil into its belly with its paws. The soil absorbs grease and grime on the fur. When the soil dries and falls off, it takes the grease and grime with it.

To avoid losing vital body heat to the cold ground, the panda usually sleeps lying on a thick patch of pine needles. It loses most heat through its head, so it rests its head on its hind legs or against the roots of a tree.

Leaving Home

Giant pandas are fully grown by the time they are three years old. By now, most pandas are completely independent. A panda's first task as an adult is to find an area of its own, where it can feed undisturbed by others.

Each adult lives in an area of 4–6 square kilometres, known as its home range. Within this is a patch measuring less than half a square kilometre, which is the panda's actual home. This is called its core area.

Adult females stay close to their core areas, but males roam widely through their home range to see which other pandas live nearby. In this way, they discover where to find the females when it is time to breed, and where their male rivals are.

▶ The best core areas have gentle slopes with a thick cover of bamboo. Older pandas usually have the best spots, so young adults have to make do with steeper slopes with less bamboo. When the older pandas die, younger ones may be able to move into their core areas.

◀ A male panda explores his home range, looking for a female to breed with.

Scent-marking

Unlike many other animals, a panda does not physically defend a territory by fighting. Instead, it uses its body scent to let other pandas know when they are entering its home range or coming close to its core area.

A panda marks the boundaries of its home range and core area by rubbing the scent glands under its tail over bushes and trees. Some trees are rubbed smooth and stained by many years of use. A male may walk backwards up a tree until he is doing a hand-stand, to make the scent mark as high up as possible.

▲ A male panda rubs his scent gland on a rock. The scent mark will let other pandas know that they are in its territory.

Strong-smelling urine sprayed on tree trunks and rocks is also used as a boundary marker, as are scratches on tree bark. All these things will tell a panda exploring a new area that other pandas are around, even if it does not see them.

▶ Even on small trees, scratch marks, sometimes very deep, are a message to other pandas.

PANDA MARKINGS

Some scientists have suggested that pandas' striking black-and-white markings enable then to see each other from afar, and avoid meetings that might result in fights.

Mating

Females are ready to breed when they are four or five years old, and males at six or seven. A female tells nearby males that she is ready to mate by calling, and probably also through changes in the smell of her scent and urine.

Males compete with each other to be her mate. This can lead to fighting, which is otherwise very rare among pandas. Males do not usually fight with their claws and teeth, but barge and bump each other in trials of strength. The fight stops when one contestant realizes that he cannot win.

▲ This wrestling match might be play, or it might have a more serious purpose. A fight for the right to mate with a female usually takes the form of bumping and barging.

The winning male tries to mate with the female. If the female does not run away, she will attack him until she decides that it is the right moment for mating. After mating, other males may then mate with her.

Mating with several males gives the female a better chance of becoming pregnant. It will also help to protect her cub. A male panda will occasionally kill a cub so that its mother needs to breed again, giving him the chance to mate with her. However, males do not kill their own cubs. If a female mates with several males, the males can never be sure that the cub she bears is not their own, and so they are less likely to kill it.

▼ A male panda (right) mates with a female (left) after winning a fight with a rival male.

Threats

Since giant pandas are so hard to study in the wild, it is not certain how many of them are left. But researchers estimate that there are probably only between 800 and 1,100 giant pandas living in the wild today in China.

The greatest threat to pandas' survival is hunting by people. Pandas are sometimes killed for their coats, which are used as rugs. Giant pandas are easy to hunt, because they are slow-moving and easy to spot in the forest.

◀ Skins of wild animals on sale in a market in Sichuan province, China. Many pandas are illegally killed for their fur each year.

In 1987, the Chinese government introduced strict laws to protect the pandas. There are severe punishments for anyone who kills pandas or who is caught selling panda skins. But the skins are so valuable that some hunters are still prepared to take the risk.

Other pandas are accidentally killed by hunters who are trying to catch musk deer and Asiatic black bears. Pandas occasionally walk into the snares that the hunters set up on forest paths. They often die before they can be released.

▲ These Chinese scientists are measuring a panda's pulse rate. Pandas are often injured by the snares set by hunters of deer and bears.

Deforestation

Giant pandas need big, old trees for dens where they can produce cubs, so they need old, undisturbed forests with good growths of bamboo. But the pandas' home is disappearing fast. China has 1,000 million people to feed and house, and there is constant pressure to cut down forests to create new farmland, and to provide firewood and timber for building.

Pandas also need to be able to move to new parts of the forest to find food when the bamboo in one area dies off. Today, these journeys are no longer possible because so much of the forest has been cut down. In 1983, at least eighty pandas starved to death after the bamboo died off in the Qionglai mountain reserve.

▲ The pandas' misty forest home is under threat from the spread of human settlements and farming.

▶ Protecting the panda's forest home will help to save many other rare plants and animals, as well as the pandas themselves.

Saving Giant Pandas

There are thirty-four giant panda reserves in China, where the pandas' forest home is protected. Together, they cover an area of more than 10,000 square kilometres. The largest reserve is at Wolong, in the mountains of eastern Sichuan. Although it has been protected since 1975, the reserve had still lost half its pandas to poachers by 1986. Despite this, the Chinese government is determined to make the reserve a success.

▼ Wolong's scientific station is the centre of Chinese panda research.

▲ A panda from the Wolong breeding centre climbs into its cage to go home after an outing in the forest.

One plan is to create 'corridors' of protected forest between the reserves. This would make it easier for the pandas to move from one reserve to another, and enable them to reach new feeding grounds when the bamboo dies off. It would also improve their chances of breeding successfully in the wild, because it would be a way of mixing males and females from different areas.

▲ Pandas always draw big crowds in zoos throughout the world.

Pandas in Zoos

To help the pandas survive, many zoos are trying to breed pandas. The first giant panda born in captivity was Ming Ming, in Beijing Zoo, China, in 1963, followed by two more in the next two years. It seemed to be the start of a great breakthrough in the battle to save the panda from extinction, but this has not been the case.

A FUTURE IN THE WILD?

Pandas born in zoos will not be released into their natural habitat until the problems that the wild pandas face have been solved. The future of the giant panda depends on the protection of the wild panda population, and its home in China's mountain forests.

Outside China, the zoos most successful at breeding pandas have been Mexico City, with four cubs that survived infancy, and Japan's Tokyo zoo, which raised two cubs. Other zoos have had some successes, but the cubs are often stillborn, or die within the first few days. Scientists are trying to discover why pandas find it so hard to breed in captivity.

On page 47 you will find the address of the World Wide Fund for Nature, which is working to save the giant panda.

▼ A mother and her young cub in the breeding centre at Chengdu, China.

Panda Life Cycle

 1 At birth, giant panda cubs are the size of rats. They are pink, blind and completely helpless. Female giant pandas may have two or three cubs, but usually only one will survive.

 2 During the first three weeks, the cub stays cradled in its mother's forepaws. After about six or eight weeks it opens its eyes, and at two-and-a-half or three months, the cub can crawl.

 3 At four months, the panda cub can walk on its own, but it will not be weaned until it is at least eight months old.

The cub stays with its mother until it is eighteen months old, and sometimes for three years or more. By three years of age, it will have reached its full adult size and weight and be completely independent.

 Female giant pandas are ready to breed at four or five years old, and males at six or seven.

 In captivity, giant pandas can live for thirty years, but in the wild they only live for up to twenty years.

GEOGRAPHY
• Mountain study
• Weather
• China

RE
• Caring for our world
• Patterns in nature

SCIENCE
• Adaptation
• Mammals
• Life cycles
• Predator/prey relationships
• Endangered species

Giant Panda Topic Web

ENGLISH
• Starting point for work on word origins
• Adjectives and descriptive writing
• Writing own stories and poems
• Mime
• Hold a debate over whether pandas should be kept in zoos.

MATHS
• Symmetry

MUSIC
• Listen to music from China

ART
• Multi-media work based on the theme 'black and white'
• Mask-making
• Camouflage

Extension Activities

English
• Develop research skills (using books and I.T.) by finding out about a range of animals featured in the text.
• Sequence the daily life of the panda.
• Read a simple story and write and perform a play.

Science
• Introduction to a study of mammals and their characteristics.
• Find out about the environmental factors that cause species to become endangered.

• Make a fact file of endangered species.

Geography
• Debate the environmental issues raised.

Music
• Compose music to accompany mime.

I.T.
• Explore ways to inform others of the plight of the species.

Glossary

Canine teeth Long, pointed teeth at the front of a giant panda's jaws, two on the top jaw and two on the bottom jaw.

Core area The place where a giant panda makes its home.

Extinct No longer existing.

False thumb A giant panda's extended wrist bone, which helps it to grip bamboo.

Home range A panda's feeding ground.

Incisor teeth Sharp teeth for cutting through flesh.

Mammal An animal that feeds its young on milk produced by the female's mammary glands.

Molars Broad teeth for grinding up food.

Parasitic worm A worm that lodges in the gut of an animal and feeds off it.

Poachers People who hunt and kill animals illegally.

Predators Animals that kill other creatures for food.

Pregnant A female animal is pregnant when a baby is developing in her womb.

Reserve A place where animals and wildlife are protected.

Scent gland A part of a panda's body that produces a smelly liquid, which the panda uses to signal to other pandas.

Snares Traps for catching animals. A snare consists of a loop of wire or cord that tightens around part of an animal's body, preventing it from escaping.

Stillborn Dead at birth.

Territory The area in which an animal, or group of animals lives, and which it defends against intruders and enemies.

Weaned When a young animal has stopped drinking its mother's milk.

Further Information

Organization to Contact

WWF-UK
Panda House, Weyside Park,
Godalming, Surrey GU7 1XR
Tel: 01483 426444
Website: www.wwf-uk.org

Websites

WWF Panda Site
www.panda.org

Everything You Need to Know About the Giant Panda
www.geocities.com/Athens/Acropolis/9492
Facts about breeding, habits, food, conservation and more.

All About Pandas
www.fonz.org/ppage.htm
Run by the Friends of the National Zoo in Washington DC. Information, a game and an animated map charting the panda's decline.

China Unique
www.chinaunique.com/Panda
Facts about China, including a section on pandas.

Books to Read

Atlas of Endangered Animals by Steve Pollock (Belitha Press, 1994)
Pandas by Karen Sullivan (Caxton Editions, 1998)
Pandas for Kids by Kathy Feeney (NorthWord Press, 1997)

Index

All the numbers in **bold** refer to photographs or illustrations.

birth 8, 42, 43, 44, 47
breeding 8, 26, 30, 34, **41**, 42, **43,** 45

calling 26, 34
China **4,** 6, **7, 11, 15**
claws 5, 13, 34
core area 30, 32, 47

den 8
drinking **25**

ears 26, **27**
extinction 4, 42, 47
eyes **5,** 12, 26, 44

false thumb **5,** 6, 47
fighting **34**
food and feeding 6, **7,** 9, 10, **12,** 14, **18, 19, 20, 21, 22,** 23, **24,** 28, **31, 39**
fur and coat 11, 26, 29, 36

golden cat 10, **11**
golden monkeys 16, **17,** 24
gut 12, 20

habitat 6, 42
head **5,** 26, **27**
home range 30, 32, 47
hunting 36, 37

jaws **5,** 37

lifespan 45
leopards 10, 16

mating 8, 26, 34, **35**
milk and suckling **9,** 10, 47
musk deer **16,** 24, 37

paws **5,** 20, 29
poachers 25, 40, 47

predators 10, **11,** 13, 16, 47
pregnancy 8, 35, 44, 47

red pandas **6,** 15
reserves 38, 40, 41, 47
rest and sleep 28, **29**

scent 25, 26, **32,** 34, 47
scratching **33**
size and weight 4, 8, 21, 44, 45
starvation 23, 38

teeth **5,** 13, 34, 47
territory 32, 47

urine 26, 32, 34

weaning 12, 44, 47

zoos 23, **42,** 43